THE *New* Palm Sunday *of the* Passion of the Lord

The New Palm Sunday of the Passion of the Lord
Published by **Redemptorist Publications**
Alphonsus House, Chawton, Hampshire, GU34 3HQ
Email rp@rpbooks.co.uk, www.rpbooks.co.uk
A registered charity limited by guarantee.
Registered in England 3261721

This compilation © Redemptorist Publications, 2014

First published 2014

General Editor: Denis McBride C.Ss.R.
Editor: Peter Edwards
Design: Rosemarie Pink

ISBN 978-0-85231-413-5

All rights reserved. No part of this publication may be reproduced, stored in a retrieval system, or transmitted in any form or by any means, electronic, mechanical, photocopying, recording or otherwise, without prior permission in writing from Redemptorist Publications.

A CIP catalogue record for this book is available from the British Library.

Acknowledgements: Excerpts from the English translation of *The Roman Missal* © 2010, International Commission on English in the Liturgy Corporation. The English translation of the Gospel Readings for the Palm Sunday Procession from the Catholic Edition of the *Revised Standard Version* of the Bible 1965, 1966 by the Division of Christian Education of the National Council of the Churches of Christ in the United States of America. The Grail Psalter (by permission of The Grail, England and HarperCollins & Co. Ltd); Bible readings are taken from the JERUSALEM BIBLE © 1966, 1967, 1968 by Darton, Longman & Todd Ltd, and Doubleday and Company Inc. and are used by permission of the Publishers. All rights reserved.

Concordat cum originali Ann Blackett
Imprimatur + Peter Doyle, Bishop of Northampton
9 December 2014.
Permission granted for distribution in dioceses of Scotland

Printed by Lithgo Press Ltd, Leicester LE8 6NU

Palm Sunday of the Passion of the Lord

THE COMMEMORATION OF THE LORD'S ENTRANCE INTO JERUSALEM

First Form: The Procession

The people, holding palm branches, gather in a place distinct from the church to which the procession will move. The following antiphon, or another suitable song, is sung:

**Hosanna to the Son of David;
blessed is he who comes in the name of the Lord,
the King of Israel.
Hosanna in the highest.**

All make the Sign of the Cross.

Priest: In the name of the Father, and of the Son, and of the Holy Spirit.
People: **Amen.**

The priest greets the people in one of the following ways:

The grace of our Lord Jesus Christ,
and the love of God,
and the communion of the Holy Spirit
be with you all.

or

Grace to you and peace from God our Father
and the Lord Jesus Christ.

or

The Lord be with you.
And with your spirit.

The priest gives a brief introduction, inviting the people to take a full part in the celebration of this day, in these or similar words:

Dear brethren (brothers and sisters),
since the beginning of Lent until now
we have prepared our hearts by penance and charitable works.
Today we gather together to herald with the whole Church
the beginning of the celebration
of our Lord's Paschal Mystery,
that is to say, of his Passion and Resurrection.
For it was to accomplish this mystery
that he entered his own city of Jerusalem.
Therefore, with all faith and devotion,
let us commemorate
the Lord's entry into the city for our salvation,
following in his footsteps,
so that, being made by his grace partakers of the Cross,
we may have a share also in his Resurrection and in his life.

Then the priest says one of the following prayers:

Let us pray.

Almighty ever-living God,
sanctify ✚ these branches with your blessing,
that we, who follow Christ the King in exultation,
may reach the eternal Jerusalem through him.
Who lives and reigns for ever and ever.
Amen.

or

Increase the faith of those who place their hope in you,
   O God,
and graciously hear the prayers of those who call on you,
that we, who today hold high these branches
to hail Christ in his triumph,
may bear fruit for you by good works accomplished in him.
Who lives and reigns for ever and ever.
Amen.

The priest sprinkles the branches with holy water.

Then the Gospel concerning the Lord's entrance is proclaimed, according to the cycle for the year:

The Lord be with you
And with your spirit.

A reading from the holy Gospel according to N.
Glory to you, O Lord.

Year A
Matthew 21:1-11

Blessed is he who comes in the name of the Lord.

When they drew near to Jerusalem and came to Bethphage, to the Mount of Olives, Jesus sent two disciples, saying to them, "Go into the village opposite you, and immediately you will find an ass tied, and a colt with her; untie them and bring them to me. If any one says anything to you, you shall say, 'The Lord has need of them,' and he will send them immediately." This took place to fulfil what was spoken by the prophet, saying,

> "Tell the daughter of Sion,
> Behold, your king is coming to you,
> humble, and mounted on an ass,
> and on a colt, the foal of an ass."

The disciples went and did as Jesus had directed them; they brought the ass and the colt, and put their garments on them, and he sat thereon. Most of the crowd spread their garments on the road, and others cut branches from the trees and spread them on the road. And the crowds that went before him and that followed him shouted,

> "Hosanna to the Son of David!
> Blessed is he who comes in the name of the Lord!
> Hosanna in the highest!"

And when he entered Jerusalem, all the city was stirred, saying, "Who is this?" And the crowds said, "This is the prophet Jesus from Nazareth of Galilee."

The Gospel of the Lord.
Praise to you, Lord Jesus Christ.

Year B
Mark 11:1-10

Blessed is he who comes in the name of the Lord.

When they drew near to Jerusalem, to Bethphage and Bethany, at the Mount of Olives, Jesus sent two of his disciples, and said to them, "Go into the village opposite you, and immediately as you enter it you will find a colt tied, on which no one has ever sat; untie it and bring it. If any one says to you, 'Why are you doing this?' say, 'The Lord has need of it and will send it back here immediately.'" And they went away, and found a colt tied at the door out in the open street; and they untied it. And those who stood there said to them, "What are you doing, untying the colt?" And they told them what Jesus had said; and they let them go. And they brought the colt to Jesus, and threw their garments on it; and he sat upon it. And many spread their garments on the road, and others spread leafy branches which they had cut from the fields. And those who went before and those who followed cried out, "Hosanna! Blessed is he who comes in the name of the Lord! Blessed is the kingdom of our father David that is coming! Hosanna in the highest!"

The Gospel of the Lord.
Praise to you, Lord Jesus Christ.

or

Year B
John 12:12-16

Blessed is he who comes in the name of the Lord.

A great crowd who had come to the feast heard that Jesus was coming to Jerusalem. So they took branches of palm trees and went out to meet him, crying, "Hosanna! Blessed is he who comes in the name of the Lord, even the king of Israel!" And Jesus found a young ass and sat upon it; as is written, "Fear not, daughter of Sion; behold, your king is coming, sitting on an ass's colt!" His disciples did not understand this at first; but when Jesus was glorified, then they remembered that this had been written of him and had been done to him.

The Gospel of the Lord.
Praise to you, Lord Jesus Christ.

Year C
Luke 19:28-40

Blessed is he who comes in the name of the Lord.

Jesus went on ahead, going up to Jerusalem. When he drew near to Bethphage and Bethany, at the mount that is called Olivet, he sent two disciples, saying, "Go into the village opposite, where on entering you will find a colt tied, on which no one has ever yet sat; untie it and bring it here. If any one asks you, 'Why are you untying it?' you shall say this, 'The Lord has need of it.'" So those who were sent went away and found it as he had told them. And as they were untying the colt, its owners said to them, "Why are you untying the colt?" And they said, "The Lord has need of it." And they brought it to Jesus, and throwing their garments on the colt they set Jesus upon it. And as he rode along they spread their garments on the road. As he was drawing near, at the descent of the Mount of Olives, the whole multitude of the disciples began to rejoice and praise God with a loud voice for all the mighty works that they had seen, saying, "Blessed is the King who comes in the name of the Lord! Peace in heaven and glory in the highest!" And some of the Pharisees in the multitude said to him, "Teacher, rebuke your disciples." He answered, "I tell you, if these were silent, the very stones would cry out."

The Gospel of the Lord.
Praise to you, Lord Jesus Christ.

After the Gospel, a brief homily may be given. Then, before the procession, an invitation may be given by the priest or another minister, in these or similar words:

Dear brethren (brothers and sisters),
like the crowds who acclaimed Jesus in Jerusalem,
let us go forth in peace.

or

Let us go forth in peace.
In the name of Christ. Amen.

The procession to the church where Mass will be celebrated then begins. During the procession, the choir and people may sing the following or other appropriate songs in honour of Christ the King.

Antiphon 1

The children of the Hebrews, carrying olive branches,
went to meet the Lord, crying out and saying:
Hosanna in the highest.

This antiphon may be repeated between the verses of the following Psalm:

Psalm 23

The LORD'S is the earth and its fullness,
the world, and those who dwell in it.
It is he who set it on the seas;
on the rivers he made it firm. (Antiphon)

Who shall climb the mountain of the LORD?
The clean of hands and pure of heart,
whose soul is not set on vain things,
who has not sworn deceitful words. (Antiphon)

Blessings from the LORD shall he receive,
and right reward from the God who saves him.
Such are the people who seek him,
who seek the face of the God of Jacob. (Antiphon)

O gates, lift high your heads,
grow higher, ancient doors.
Let him enter, the king of glory!
Who is this king of glory?
The LORD, the mighty, the valiant;
the LORD, the valiant in war. (Antiphon)

O gates, lift high your heads;
grow higher, ancient doors.
Let him enter, the king of glory!
Who is this king of glory?
He, the LORD of hosts,
he is the king of glory. (Antiphon)

Antiphon 2

**The children of the Hebrews spread their garments on the road,
crying out and saying: Hosanna to the Son of David;
blessed is he who comes in the name of the Lord.**

This antiphon may be repeated between the verses of the following Psalm:

Psalm 46

All peoples, clap your hands.
Cry to God with shouts of joy!
For the LORD, the Most High, is awesome,
the great king over all the earth. (Antiphon)

He humbles peoples under us
and nations under our feet.
Our heritage he chose for us,
the pride of Jacob whom he loves.
God goes up with shouts of joy.
The LORD goes up with trumpet blast. (Antiphon)

Sing praise for God; sing praise!
Sing praise to our king; sing praise!
God is king of all earth.
Sing praise with all your skill. (Antiphon)

God reigns over the nations.
God sits upon his holy throne.
The princes of the peoples are assembled
with the people of the God of Abraham.
The rulers of the earth belong to God,
who is greatly exalted. (Antiphon)

Hymn to Christ the King

Response: **Glory and honour and praise be to you, Christ, King and Redeemer, to whom young children cried out loving Hosannas with joy.**

Israel's King are you, King David's magnificent offspring;
you are the ruler who come blest in the name of the Lord. R.

Heavenly hosts on high unite in singing your praises;
men and women on earth and all creation join in. R.

Bearing branches of palm, Hebrews came crowding to greet you;
see how with prayers and hymns we come to pay you our vows. R.

They offered gifts of praise to you, so near to your Passion;
see how we sing this song now to you reigning on high. R.

Those you were pleased to accept; now accept our gifts of devotion,
good and merciful King, lover of all that is good. R.

As the procession enters the church, the following responsory or another song that refers to the Lord's entrance is sung.

As the Lord entered the holy city, the children of the Hebrews proclaimed the resurrection of life. Waving their branches of palm, they cried: Hosanna in the Highest.

When the people heard that Jesus was coming to Jerusalem, they went out to meet him. Waving their branches of palm, they cried: Hosanna in the Highest.

Then the Mass continues with the Collect, p. 16.

Second Form: The Solemn Entrance

If the procession outside the church cannot take place, the entrance of the Lord is celebrated inside the church before the principal Mass.

The people, holding palm branches, gather either outside, in front of the church door, or inside the church. The priest and ministers and a representative group of the faithful go to a suitable place in the church outside the sanctuary, so that most of the people can see the rite.

While the priest approaches the appointed place, the antiphon Hosanna (p. 3) or another appropriate song is sung. Then the blessing of branches and the proclamation of the Gospel of the Lord's entrance into Jerusalem take place as above (pp. 4-8).

After the Gospel, the priest processes solemnly with the ministers and the representative group of the faithful through the church to the sanctuary, while the responsory As the Lord entered (p. 12) or another appropriate song is sung.

Then the Mass continues with the Collect, p. 16.

Third Form: The Simple Entrance

At all other Masses of this Sunday, if the Solemn Entrance is not held, the commemoration of the Lord's entrance into Jerusalem takes place by means of a Simple Entrance.

While the priest proceeds to the altar, the Entrance Antiphon (see below) or another song with the same theme is sung, and the Mass continues in the usual way.

At other Masses, in which singing at the entrance cannot take place, the priest, as soon as he has arrived at the altar and venerated it, greets the people, reads the Entrance Antiphon, and continues the Mass in the usual way.

Entrance Antiphon

Six days before the Passover,
when the Lord came into the city of Jerusalem,
the children ran to meet him;
in their hands they carried palm branches
and with a loud voice cried out:

Hosanna in the highest!
Blessed are you, who have come in your abundant mercy!

O gates, lift high your heads;
grow higher, ancient doors.
Let him enter, the king of glory!
Who is this king of glory?
He, the Lord of hosts, he is the king of glory.

Hosanna in the highest!
Blessed are you, who have come in your abundant mercy!

All make the Sign of the Cross.

In the name of the Father, and of the Son, and of the Holy Spirit.
Amen.

The priest greets the people in one of the following ways:

The grace of our Lord Jesus Christ,
and the love of God,
and the communion of the Holy Spirit
be with you all.

or

Grace to you and peace from God our Father
and the Lord Jesus Christ.

or

The Lord be with you.
And with your spirit.

The priest may briefly introduce the Mass.

Penitential Act

The priest invites the people to penitence.
The Penitential Act takes one of the following forms:

**I confess to almighty God
and to you, my brothers and sisters,
that I have greatly sinned,
in my thoughts and in my words,
in what I have done and in what I have failed to do,**

All strike their breast and say:

**through my fault, through my fault,
through my most grievous fault;**

**therefore I ask blessed Mary ever-Virgin,
all the Angels and Saints,
and you, my brothers and sisters,
to pray for me to the Lord our God.**

or

Have mercy on us, O Lord.
For we have sinned against you.

Show us, O Lord, your mercy.
And grant us your salvation.

or (using these or similar words):

You were sent to heal the contrite of heart:

| Lord, have mercy. | or | Kyrie, eleison. |
| **Lord, have mercy.** | | **Kyrie, eleison.** |

You came to call sinners:

| Christ, have mercy. | or | Christe, eleison. |
| **Christ, have mercy.** | | **Christe, eleison.** |

You are seated at the right hand of the Father to intercede for us:

Lord, have mercy.   or   Kyrie, eleison.
Lord, have mercy.   **Kyrie, eleison.**

The absolution by the priest follows:

May almighty God have mercy on us,
forgive us our sins,
and bring us to everlasting life.
Amen.

The Kyrie, eleison (Lord, have mercy) invocations follow, unless they have already occurred as part of the Penitential Act.

Lord, have mercy.   **Lord, have mercy.**
Christ, have mercy.   **Christ, have mercy.**
Lord, have mercy.   **Lord, have mercy.**

or

Kyrie, eleison.   **Kyrie, eleison.**
Christe, eleison.   **Christe, eleison.**
Kyrie, eleison.   **Kyrie, eleison.**

AT THE MASS
Collect

Almighty ever-living God,
who as an example of humility for the human race to follow
caused our Saviour to take flesh and submit to the Cross,
graciously grant that we may heed his lesson of patient
    suffering
and so merit a share in his Resurrection.
Who lives and reigns with you in the unity of the Holy
    Spirit,
one God, for ever and ever.
Amen.

THE LITURGY OF THE WORD
First Reading (Isaiah 50:4-7)

A reading from the prophet Isaiah.
I did not cover my face against insult – I know I shall not be shamed.

The Lord has given me
a disciple's tongue.
So that I may know how to reply to the wearied
he provides me with speech.
Each morning he wakes me to hear,
to listen like a disciple.
The Lord has opened my ear.
For my part, I made no resistance,
neither did I turn away.
I offered my back to those who struck me,
my cheeks to those who tore at my beard;
I did not cover my face
against insult and spittle.
The Lord comes to my help,
so that I am untouched by the insults.
So, too, I set my face like flint;
I know I shall not be shamed.

The word of the Lord.
Thanks be to God.

Psalm (Psalm 21)

Response: **My God, my God, why have you forsaken me?**

1. All who see me deride me.
   They curl their lips, they toss their heads.
   "He trusted in the Lord, let him save him;
   let him release him if this is his friend." R.

2. Many dogs have surrounded me,
   a band of the wicked beset me.
   They tear holes in my hands and my feet.
   I can count every one of my bones. R.

3. They divide my clothing among them.
   They cast lots for my robe.
   O Lord, do not leave me alone,
   my strength, make haste to help me! R.

4. I will tell of your name to my brethren
   and praise you where they are assembled.
   "You who fear the Lord give him praise;
   all sons of Jacob, give him glory.
   Revere him, Israel's sons." R.

Second Reading (Philippians 2:6-11)

A reading from the letter of St Paul to the Philippians.
He humbled himself, but God raised him high.

His state was divine,
yet Christ Jesus did not cling
to his equality with God
but emptied himself
to assume the condition of a slave,
and became as men are;
and being as all men are,
he was humbler yet,
even to accepting death,
death on a cross.
But God raised him high
and gave him the name
which is above all other names
so that all beings
in the heavens, on earth and in the underworld,
should bend the knee at the name of Jesus
and that every tongue should acclaim
Jesus Christ as Lord,
to the glory of God the Father.

The word of the Lord.
Thanks be to God.

Gospel Acclamation

**Praise to you, O Christ, king of eternal glory:
Christ was humbler yet,
even to accepting death, death on a cross.
But God raised him high
and gave him the name which is above all names.
Praise to you, O Christ, king of eternal glory.**

The Passion of Year A, B (p. 36) or C (p. 52) is read according to the cycle for the year. The Passion may be read by different people.

N. Narrator; J. Jesus; O. other single speaker and C. Crowd, or more than one speaker.

The usual greeting and signing of the book are omitted.

Year A
Gospel (Matthew 26:14 – 27:66)

The passion of our Lord Jesus Christ according to Matthew.

N. One of the Twelve, the man called Judas Iscariot, went to the chief priests and said,

O. "What are you prepared to give me if I hand him over to you?"

N. They paid him thirty silver pieces, and from that moment he looked for an opportunity to betray him.

Now on the first day of Unleavened Bread the disciples came to Jesus to say,

C. "Where do you want us to make the preparations for you to eat the Passover?"

N. He replied:

J. "Go to so-and-so in the city and say to him, 'The Master says: My time is near. It is at your house that I am keeping Passover with my disciples.'"

N. The disciples did what Jesus told them and prepared the Passover.

When the evening came he was at table with the twelve disciples. And while they were eating he said:

J. "I tell you solemnly, one of you is about to betray me."

N. They were greatly distressed and started asking him in turn,

C. "Not I, Lord, surely?"

N. He answered:

J. "Someone who has dipped his hand into the dish with me, will betray me. The Son of Man is going to his fate, as the scriptures say he will, but alas for that man by whom the Son of Man is betrayed! Better for that man if he had never been born!"

N. Judas, who was to betray him, asked in his turn,

O. "Not I, Rabbi, surely?"

N. Jesus answered,

J. "They are your own words."

N. Now as they were eating, Jesus took some

bread, and when he had said the blessing he broke it and gave it to the disciples and said:

J. "Take it and eat; this is my body."

N. Then he took a cup, and when he had returned thanks he gave it to them, saying:

J. "Drink all of you from this, for this is my blood, the blood of the covenant, which is to be poured out for many for the forgiveness of sins. From now on, I tell you, I shall not drink wine until the day I drink the new wine with you in the kingdom of my Father."

N. After psalms had been sung they left for the Mount of Olives. Then Jesus said to them,

J. "You will all lose faith in me this night, for the scripture says: I shall strike the shepherd and the sheep of the flock will be scattered. But after my resurrection I shall go before you to Galilee."

N. At this, Peter said,

O. "Though all lose faith in you, I will never lose faith."

N. Jesus answered him,

J. "I tell you solemnly, this very night, before the cock crows, you will have disowned me three times."

N. Peter said to him,

O. "Even if I have to die with you, I will never disown you."

N. And all the disciples said the same.
    Then Jesus came with them to a small estate called Gethsemane; and he said to his disciples,

J. "Stay here while I go over there to pray."

N. He took Peter and the two sons of Zebedee with him. And sadness came over him, and great distress. Then he said them:

J. "My soul is sorrowful to the point of death. Wait here and keep awake with me."

N. And going on a little further he fell on his face and prayed:

J. "My Father, if it is possible let this cup pass me by. Nevertheless, let it be as you, not I, would have it."

N. He came back to the disciples and found them sleeping, and he said to Peter:

J. "So you had not the strength to keep awake with me one hour? You should be awake, and praying not to be put to the test. The spirit is willing, but the flesh is weak."

N. Again, a second time, he went away and prayed:

J. "My Father, if this cup cannot pass by without my drinking it, your will be done!"

N. And he came back again and found them sleeping, their eyes were so heavy. Leaving them there, he went away again and prayed for the third time, repeating the same words. Then he came back to the disciples and said to them,

J. "You can sleep on now and take your rest. Now the hour has come when the Son of Man is to be betrayed into the hands of sinners. Get up! Let us go! My betrayer is already close at hand."

N. He was still speaking when Judas, one of the Twelve, appeared, and with him a large number of men armed with swords and clubs, sent by the chief priests and elders of the people. Now the traitor had arranged a sign with them. He had said,

O. "The one I kiss, he is the man. Take him in charge."

N. So he went straight up to Jesus and said,

O. "Greetings, Rabbi,"

N. and kissed him. Jesus said to him,

J. "My friend, do what you are here for."

N. Then they came forward, seized Jesus and took him in charge. At that, one of the followers of Jesus grasped his sword and drew it; he struck out at the high priest's servant, and cut off his ear. Jesus then said:

J. "Put your sword back, for all who draw the sword will die by the sword. Or do you think that I cannot appeal to my Father who would

N. promptly send more than twelve legions of angels to my defence? But then, how would the scriptures be fulfilled that say this is the way it must be?"

N. It was at this time that Jesus said to the crowds:

J. "Am I a brigand, that you had to set out to capture me with swords and clubs? I sat teaching in the Temple day after day and you never laid hands on me."

N. Now all this happened to fulfil the prophecies in scripture. Then all the disciples deserted him and ran away.

The men who had arrested Jesus led him off to Caiaphas the high priest, where the scribes and the elders were assembled. Peter followed him at a distance, and when he reached the high priest's palace, he went in and sat down with the attendants to see what the end would be.

The chief priests and the whole Sanhedrin were looking for evidence against Jesus, however false, on which they might pass the death-sentence. But they could not find any, though several lying witnesses came forward. Eventually two stepped forward and made a statement,

O. "This man said: 'I have power to destroy the Temple of God and in three days build it up.'"

N. The high priest then stood up and said to him:

O. "Have you no answer to that? What is this evidence these men are bringing against you?"

N. But Jesus was silent. And the high priest said to him:

O. "I put you on oath by the living God to tell us if you are the Christ, the Son of God."

N. Jesus answered:

J. "The words are your own. Moreover, I tell you that from this time onward you will see the Son of Man seated at the right hand of the Power and coming on the clouds of heaven."

N. At this, the high priest tore his clothes and said:

O. "He has blasphemed. What need of witnesses have we now? There! You have just heard the blasphemy. What is your opinion?"

N. They answered,

C. "He deserves to die."

N. Then they spat in his face and hit him with their fists; others said as they struck him:

C. "Play the prophet, Christ! Who hit you then?"

N. Meanwhile Peter was sitting outside in the courtyard, and a servant-girl came up to him and said:

O. "You too were with Jesus the Galilean."

N. But he denied it in front of them all, saying:

O. "I do not know what you are talking about."

N. When he went out to the gateway another servant-girl saw him and said to the people there:

O. "This man was with Jesus the Nazarene."

N. And again, with an oath, he denied it,

O. "I do not know the man."

N. A little later the bystanders came up and said to Peter:

C. "You are one of them for sure! Why, your accent gives you away."

N. Then he started calling down curses on himself and swearing:

O. "I do not know the man."

N. At that moment the cock crew, and Peter remembered what Jesus had said, "Before the cock crows you will have disowned me three times." And he went outside and wept bitterly.

When morning came, all the chief priests and the elders of the people met in council to bring about the death of Jesus. They had him bound, and led him away to hand him over to Pilate, the governor. When he found that Jesus had been condemned, Judas his betrayer was filled with remorse and took the thirty pieces of silver back to the chief priests and elders, saying:

O. "I have sinned. I have betrayed innocent blood."

N. They replied:

C. "What is that to us? That is your concern."

N. And flinging down the silver pieces in the sanctuary he made off, and went and hanged himself. The chief priests picked up the silver pieces and said:

C. "It is against the Law to put this into the treasury; it is blood money."

N. So they discussed the matter and bought the potter's field with it as a graveyard for foreigners, and this is why the field is called the Field of Blood today. The words of the prophet Jeremiah were then fulfilled: And they took the thirty silver pieces, the sum at which the precious One was priced by children of Israel, and they gave them for the potter's field, just as the Lord directed me.

Jesus, then, was brought before the governor, and the governor put to him this question:

O. "Are you the king of the Jews?"

N. Jesus replied:

J. "It is you who say it."

N. But when he was accused by the chief priests and the elders he refused to answer at all. Pilate then said to him:

O. "Do you not hear how many charges they have brought against you?"

N. But to the governor's complete amazement, he offered no reply to any of the charges.

At festival time it was the governor's practice to release a prisoner for the people, anyone they chose. Now there was at that time a notorious prisoner whose name was Barabbas. So when the crowd gathered, Pilate said to them,

O. "Which do you want me to release for you: Barabbas, or Jesus who is called Christ?"

N. For Pilate knew it was out of jealousy that they had handed him over. Now as he was seated in the chair of judgement, his wife sent him a message,

O. "Have nothing to do with that man; I have been upset all day by a dream I had about him."

N. The chief priests and the elders, however, had persuaded the crowd to demand the release of Barabbas and the execution of Jesus. So when the governor spoke and asked them:

O. "Which of the two do you want me to release for you?"

N. they said:

C. "Barabbas."

N. Pilate said to them:

O. "What am I to do with Jesus who is called Christ?"

N. They all said:

C. "Let him be crucified!"

N. Pilate asked:

O. "Why? What harm has he done?"

N. But they shouted all the louder,

C. "Let him be crucified!"

N. Then Pilate saw that he was making no impression, that in fact a riot was imminent. So he took some water, washed his hands in front of the crowd and said:

O. "I am innocent of this man's blood. It is your concern."

N. And the people, to a man, shouted back:

C. "His blood be on us and on our children!"

N. Then he released Barabbas for them. He ordered Jesus to be first scourged and then handed over to be crucified.

The governor's soldiers took Jesus with them into the Praetorium and collected the whole cohort round him. Then they stripped him and made him wear a scarlet cloak, and having twisted some thorns into a crown they put this on his head and placed a reed in his right hand. To make fun of him they knelt to him saying:

C. "Hail, king of the Jews!"

N. And they spat on him and took the reed and struck him on the head with it. And when they had finished making fun of him, they took off the cloak and dressed him in his own clothes and led him away to crucify him.

On their way out, they came across a man from Cyrene, Simon by name, and enlisted him to carry his cross. When they had reached a place called Golgotha, that is, the place of the skull, they gave him wine to drink mixed with gall, which he tasted but refused to drink. When they had finished crucifying him they shared out his clothing by casting lots, and then sat down and stayed there keeping guard over him. Above his head was placed the charge against him; it read: "This is Jesus, the King of the Jews." At the same time two robbers were crucified with him, one on the right and one on the left.

The passers-by jeered at him; they shook their heads and said:

C. "So you would destroy the Temple and rebuild it in three days! Then save yourself! If you are God's son, come down from the cross!"

N. The chief priests with the scribes and elders mocked him in the same way, saying,

C. "He saved others; he cannot save himself. He is the King of Israel; let him come down from the cross now, and we will believe in him. He put his trust in God; now let God rescue him if he wants him. For he did say, 'I am the son of God.'"

N. Even the robbers who were crucified with him taunted him in the same way.

From the sixth hour there was darkness over all the land until the ninth hour. And about the ninth hour, Jesus cried out in a loud voice:

J. "Eli, Eli, lama sabachthani?"

N. That is: "My God, my God, why have you deserted me?" When some of those who stood there heard this, they said:

C. "The man is calling on Elijah,"

N. and one of them quickly ran to get a sponge which he dipped in vinegar and, putting it on a reed, gave it him to drink. The rest of them said:

C. "Wait! See if Elijah will come to save him."

N. But Jesus, again crying out in a loud voice, yielded up his spirit.

All kneel and pause for a moment.

N. At that, the veil of the Temple was torn in two from top to bottom; the earth quaked; the rocks were split; the tombs opened and the bodies of many holy men rose from the dead, and these, after his resurrection, came out of the tombs, entered the Holy City and appeared to a number of people.

    Meanwhile the centurion, together with the others guarding Jesus, had seen the earthquake and all that was taking place, and they were terrified and said:

C. "In truth this was a son of God."

N. And many women were there, watching from a distance, the same women who had followed Jesus from Galilee and looked after him. Among them were Mary of Magdala, Mary the mother of James and Joseph, and the mother of Zebedee's sons.

    When it was evening, there came a rich man of Arimathaea, called Joseph, who had himself become a disciple of Jesus. This man went to Pilate and asked for the body of Jesus. Pilate thereupon ordered it to be handed over. So Joseph took the body, wrapped it in a clean shroud and put it in his own new tomb which he had hewn out of the rock. He then rolled a large stone across the entrance of the tomb and went away. Now Mary of Magdala and the other Mary were there, sitting opposite the sepulchre.

    Next day, that is, when Preparation Day was over, the chief priests and the Pharisees went in a body to Pilate and said to him,

C. "Your Excellency, we recall that this impostor said, while he was still alive, 'After three days I shall rise again.' Therefore give the order to have the sepulchre kept secure until the third day, for fear his disciples come and steal him away and tell the people, 'He has risen from the dead.' This last piece of fraud would be worse than what went before."

N. Pilate said to them:

O. "You may have your guards. Go and make all as secure as you know how."

N. So they went and made the sepulchre secure, putting seals on the stone and mounting a guard.

The Gospel of the Lord.
Praise to you, Lord Jesus Christ.

This shorter alternative may be read instead:

Gospel (Matthew 27:11-54)

The passion of our Lord Jesus Christ according to Matthew.

Jesus was brought before Pontius Pilate, the governor, and the governor put to him this question, "Are you the king of the Jews?" Jesus replied, "It is you who say it." But when he was accused by the chief priests and the elders he refused to answer at all. Pilate then said to him, "Do you not hear how many charges they have brought against you?" But to the governor's complete amazement, he offered no reply to any of the charges.

At festival time it was the governor's practice to release a prisoner for the people, anyone they chose. Now there was at that time a notorious prisoner whose name was Barabbas. So when the crowd gathered, Pilate said to them, "Which do you want me to release for you: Barabbas, or Jesus who is called Christ?" For Pilate knew it was out of jealousy that they had handed him over.

Now as he was seated in the chair of judgement, his wife sent him a message, "Have nothing to do with that man; I have been upset all day by a dream I had about him."

The chief priests and the elders, however, had persuaded the crowd to demand the release of Barabbas and the execution of Jesus. So when the governor spoke and asked them: "Which of the two do you want me to release for you?" they said, "Barabbas." "But in that case," Pilate said to them, "what am I to do with Jesus who is called Christ?" They all said, "Let him be crucified!" "Why?" he asked, "What harm has he done?" But they shouted all the louder, "Let him be crucified!" Then Pilate saw that he was making no impression, that in fact a riot was imminent. So he took some water, washed his hands in front of the crowd and said, "I am innocent of this man's blood. It is your concern." And the people, to a man, shouted back, "His blood be on us and on our children!" Then he released Barabbas for them. He ordered Jesus to be first scourged and then handed over to be crucified.

The governor's soldiers took Jesus with them into the Praetorium and collected the whole cohort round him. Then they stripped him and made him wear a scarlet cloak, and having twisted some thorns into a crown they put this on his head and placed a reed in his right hand. To make fun of him they knelt to him saying: "Hail, king of the

Jews!" And they spat on him and took the reed and struck him on the head with it. And when they had finished making fun of him, they took off the cloak and dressed him in his own clothes and led him away to crucify him.

On their way out, they came across a man from Cyrene, Simon by name, and enlisted him to carry his cross. When they had reached a place called Golgotha, that is, the place of the skull, they gave him wine to drink mixed with gall, which he tasted but refused to drink. When they had finished crucifying him they shared out his clothing by casting lots, and then sat down and stayed there keeping guard over him.

Above his head was placed the charge against him; it read: "This is Jesus, the King of the Jews." At the same time two robbers were crucified with him, one on the right and one on the left.

The passers-by jeered at him; they shook their heads and said, "So you would destroy the Temple and rebuild it in three days! Then save yourself! If you are God's son, come down from the cross!" The chief priests with the scribes and elders mocked him in the same way. "He saved others," they said, "he cannot save himself. He is the King of Israel; let him come down from the cross now, and we will believe in him. He put his trust in God; now let God rescue him if he wants him. For he did say, 'I am the son of God.'" Even the robbers who were crucified with him taunted him in the same way.

From the sixth hour there was darkness over all the land until the ninth hour. And about the ninth hour, Jesus cried out in a loud voice: "Eli, Eli, lama sabachthani?" that is: "My God, my God, why have you deserted me?" When some of those who stood there heard this, they said: "The man is calling on Elijah," and one of them quickly ran to get a sponge which he dipped in vinegar and, putting it on a reed, gave it him to drink. "Wait!" said the rest of them, "and see if Elijah will come to save him." But Jesus, again crying out in a loud voice, yielded up his spirit.

All kneel and pause for a moment.

At that, the veil of the Temple was torn in two from top to bottom; the earth quaked; the rocks were split; the tombs opened and the bodies of many holy men rose from the dead, and these, after his resurrection, came out of the tombs, entered the Holy City and appeared to a number of people.

Meanwhile the centurion, together with the others guarding Jesus, had seen the earthquake and all that was taking place, and they were terrified and said: "In truth this was a son of God."

The Gospel of the Lord.
Praise to you, Lord Jesus Christ.

Year B
Gospel (Mark 14:1 – 15:47)

The passion of our Lord Jesus Christ according to Mark.

N. It was two days before the Passover and the

feast of Unleavened Bread, and the chief priests and scribes were looking for a way to arrest Jesus by some trick and have him put to death. For they said,

C. "It must not be during the festivities, or there will be a disturbance among the people."

N. Jesus was at Bethany in the house of Simon the leper; he was at dinner when a woman came in with an alabaster jar of very costly ointment, pure nard. She broke the jar and poured the ointment on his head. Some who were there said to one another indignantly,

C. "Why this waste of ointment? Ointment like this could have been sold for over three hundred denarii and the money given to the poor,"

N. and they were angry with her. But Jesus said,

J. "Leave her alone. Why are you upsetting her? What she has done for me is one of the good works. You have the poor with you always, and you can be kind to them whenever you wish, but you will not always have me. She has done what was in her power to do; she has anointed my body beforehand for its burial. I tell you solemnly, wherever throughout all the world the Good News is proclaimed, what she has done will be told also, in remembrance of her."

N. Judas Iscariot, one of the Twelve, approached the chief priests with an offer to hand Jesus over to them. They were delighted to hear it, and promised to give him money; and he looked for a way of betraying him when the opportunity should occur.

On the first day of Unleavened Bread, when the Passover lamb was sacrificed, his disciples said to him,

C. "Where do you want us to go and make the preparations for you to eat the Passover?"

N. So he sent two of his disciples, saying to them,

J. "Go into the city and you will meet a man carrying a pitcher of water. Follow him, and say to the owner of the house which he enters, 'The Master says: Where is my dining room in which I can eat the Passover with my disciples?' He will show you a large upper room furnished with couches, all prepared. Make the preparations for us there."

N. The disciples set out and went to the city and found everything as he had told them, and prepared the Passover.

When evening came he arrived with the Twelve. And while they were at table eating, Jesus said,

J. "I tell you solemnly, one of you is about to betray me, one of you eating with me."

N. They were distressed and asked him, one after another,

O. "Not I, surely?"

N. He said to them,

J. "It is one of the Twelve, one who is dipping into the same dish with me. Yes, the Son of Man is going to his fate, as the scriptures say he will, but alas for that man by whom the Son of Man is betrayed! Better for that man if he had never been born!"

N. And as they were eating he took some bread, and when he had said the blessing he broke it and gave it to them, saying,

J. "Take it; this is my body."

N. Then he took a cup, and when he had returned thanks he gave it to them, and all drank from it, and he said to them,

J. "This is my blood, the blood of the covenant, which is to be poured out for many. I tell you solemnly, I shall not drink any more wine until the day I drink the new wine in the kingdom of God."

N. After psalms had been sung they left for the Mount of Olives. And Jesus said to them,

J. "You will all lose faith, for the scripture says, 'I shall strike the shepherd and the sheep will be scattered'. However after my resurrection I shall go before you to Galilee."

N. Peter said,

O. "Even if all lose faith, I will not."

N. And Jesus said to him,

J. "I tell you solemnly, this day, this very night, before the cock crows twice, you will have disowned me three times."

N. But he repeated still more earnestly,

O. "If I have to die with you, I will never disown you."

N. And they all said the same.
   They came to a small estate called Gethsemane, and Jesus said to his disciples,

J. "Stay here while I pray."

N. Then he took Peter and James and John with him. And a sudden fear came over him, and great distress. And he said to them,

J. "My soul is sorrowful to the point of death. Wait here, and keep awake."

N. And going on a little further he threw himself on the ground and prayed that, if it were possible, this hour might pass him by. He said,

J. "Abba (Father)! Everything is possible for you. Take this cup away from me. But let it be as you, not I, would have it."

N. He came back and found them sleeping, and he said to Peter,

J. "Simon, are you asleep? Had you not the strength to keep awake one hour? You should be awake, and praying not to be put to the test. The spirit is willing but the flesh is weak."

N. Again he went away and prayed, saying the same words. And once more he came back and found them sleeping, their eyes were so heavy; and they could find no answer for him. He came back a third time and said to them,

J. "You can sleep on now and take your rest. It is all over. The hour has come. Now the Son of Man is to be betrayed into the hands of sinners. Get up! Let us go! My betrayer is close at hand already."

N. Even while he was still speaking, Judas, one of the Twelve, came up with a number of men armed with swords and clubs, sent by the chief priests and the scribes and the elders. Now the traitor had arranged a signal with them. He had said,

O. "The one I kiss, he is the man. Take him in charge, and see he is well guarded when you lead him away."

N. So when the traitor came, he went straight up to Jesus and said,

O. "Rabbi!"

N. and kissed him. The others seized him and took him in charge. Then one of the bystanders drew his sword and struck out at the high priest's servant, and cut off his ear.
   Then Jesus spoke,

J. "Am I a brigand that you had to set out to capture me with swords and clubs? I was among you teaching in the Temple day after day and you never laid hands on me. But this is to fulfil the scriptures."

N. And they all deserted him and ran away. A young man who followed him had nothing on but a linen cloth. They caught hold of him, but he left the cloth in their hands and ran away naked.

    They led Jesus off to the high priest; and all the chief priests and the elders and the scribes assembled there. Peter had followed him at a distance, right into the high priest's palace, and was sitting with the attendants warming himself at the fire.

    The chief priests and the whole Sanhedrin were looking for evidence against Jesus on which they might pass the death-sentence. But they could not find any. Several, indeed, brought false evidence against him, but their evidence was conflicting. Some stood up and submitted this false evidence against him,

C. "We heard him say, 'I am going to destroy this Temple made by human hands, and in three days build another, not made by human hands.'"

N. But even on this point their evidence was conflicting. The high priest then stood up before the whole assembly and put this question to Jesus,

O. "Have you no answer to that? What is this evidence these men are bringing against you?"

N. But he was silent and made no answer at all. The high priest put a second question to him,

O. "Are you the Christ, the Son of the Blessed One?"

N. Jesus said,

J. "I am, and you will see the Son of Man seated at the right hand of the Power and coming with the clouds of heaven."

N. The high priest tore his robes, and said,

O. "What need of witnesses have we now? You heard the blasphemy. What is your finding?"

N. And they all gave their verdict: he deserved to die. Some of them started spitting at him and, blindfolding him, began hitting him with their fists and shouting,

C. "Play the prophet!"

N. And the attendants rained blows on him.
   While Peter was down below in the courtyard, one of the high priest's servant-girls came up. She saw Peter warming himself there, stared at him and said,

O. "You too were with Jesus, the man from Nazareth."

N. But he denied it, saying,

O. "I do not know, I do not understand what you are talking about."

N. And he went out into the forecourt. The servant-girl saw him and again started telling the bystanders,

O. "This fellow is one of them."

N. But he again denied it. A little later the bystanders themselves said to Peter,

C. "You are one of them for sure! Why, you are a Galilean."

N. But he started calling curses on himself and swearing,

O. "I do not know the man you speak of."

N. At that moment the cock crew for the second time, and Peter recalled how Jesus had said to him, "Before the cock crows twice, you will have disowned me three times." And he burst into tears.

First thing in the morning, the chief priests together with the elders and scribes, in short the whole Sanhedrin, had their plan ready. They had Jesus bound and took him away and handed him over to Pilate.

Pilate questioned him,

O. "Are you the king of the Jews?"

N. He answered,

J. "It is you who say it."

N. And the chief priests brought many accusations against him. Pilate questioned him again,

O. "Have you no reply at all? See how many accusations they are bringing against you!"

N. But to Pilate's amazement, Jesus made no further reply.

At festival time Pilate used to release a prisoner for them, anyone they asked for. Now a man called Barabbas was then in prison with the rioters who had committed murder during the uprising. When the crowd went up and began to ask Pilate the customary favour, Pilate answered them,

O. "Do you want me to release for you the king of the Jews?"

N. For he realised it was out of jealousy that the chief priests had handed Jesus over. The chief priests, however, had incited the crowd to demand that he should release Barabbas for them instead. Then Pilate spoke again.

O. "But in that case, what am I to do with the man you call king of the Jews?"

N. They shouted back,

C. "Crucify him!"

N. Pilate asked them,

O. "Why? What harm has he done?"

N. But they shouted all the louder,

C. "Crucify him!"

N. So Pilate, anxious to placate the crowd, released Barabbas for them and, having ordered Jesus to be scourged, handed him over to be crucified.

The soldiers led him away to the inner part of the palace, that is, the Praetorium, and called the whole cohort together. They dressed him up in purple, twisted some thorns into a crown and put it on him. And they began saluting him,

C. "Hail, king of the Jews!"

N. They struck his head with a reed and spat on him; and they went down on their knees to do him homage. And when they had finished making fun of him, they took off the purple and dressed him in his own clothes.

They led him out to crucify him. They enlisted a passer-by, Simon of Cyrene, father of Alexander and Rufus, who was coming in from the country, to carry his cross. They brought Jesus to the place called Golgotha, which means the place of the skull.

They offered him wine mixed with myrrh, but he refused it. Then they crucified him, and shared out his clothing, casting lots to decide what each should get. It was the third hour when they crucified him. The inscription giving the charge against him read: "The King of the Jews." And they crucified two robbers with him, one on his right and one on his left.

The passers-by jeered at him; they shook their heads and said,

C. "Aha! So you would destroy the Temple and rebuild it in three days! Then save yourself: come down from the cross!"

N. The chief priests and the scribes mocked him among themselves in the same way. They said,

C. "He saved others, he cannot save himself. Let the Christ, the king of Israel, come down from the cross now, for us to see it and believe."

N. Even those who were crucified with him taunted him.

When the sixth hour came there was darkness over the whole land until the ninth hour. And at the ninth hour Jesus cried out in a loud voice,

J. "Eloi, Eloi, lama sabachthani?"

N. This means "My God, my God, why have you deserted me?" When some of those who stood by heard this, they said,

C. "Listen, he is calling on Elijah."

N. Someone ran and soaked a sponge in vinegar and, putting it on a reed, gave it him to drink, saying,

O. "Wait and see if Elijah will come to take him down."

N. But Jesus gave a loud cry and breathed his last.

All kneel and pause for a moment.

N. And the veil of the Temple was torn in two from top to bottom. The centurion, who was standing in front of him, had seen how he had died, and he said,

O. "In truth this man was a son of God."

N. There were some women watching from a distance. Among them were Mary of Magdala, Mary who was the mother of James the younger and Joset, and Salome. These used to follow him and look after him when he was in Galilee. And there were many other women there who had come up to Jerusalem with him.

   It was now evening, and since it was Preparation Day (that is, the vigil of the sabbath), there came Joseph of Arimathaea, a prominent member of the Council, who himself lived in the hope of seeing the kingdom of God, and he boldly went to Pilate and asked for the body of Jesus. Pilate, astonished that he should have died so soon, summoned the centurion and enquired if he was already dead. Having been assured of this by the centurion, he granted the corpse to Joseph who brought a shroud, took Jesus down from the cross, wrapped him in the shroud and laid him in a tomb which had been hewn out of the rock. He then rolled a stone against the entrance to the tomb. Mary of Magdala and Mary the mother of Joset were watching and took note of where he was laid.

The Gospel of the Lord.
Praise to you, Lord Jesus Christ.

This shorter alternative may be read instead:

Gospel (Mark 15:1-39)

The passion of our Lord Jesus Christ according to Mark.

First thing in the morning, the chief priests together with the elders and scribes, in short the whole Sanhedrin, had their plan ready. They had Jesus bound and took him away and handed him over to Pilate.

Pilate questioned him, "Are you the king of the Jews?" "It is you who say it" he answered. And the chief priests brought many accusations against him. Pilate questioned him again, "Have you no reply at all? See how many accusations they are bringing against you!" But to Pilate's amazement, Jesus made no further reply.

At festival time Pilate used to release a prisoner for them, anyone they asked for. Now a man called Barabbas was then in prison with the rioters who had committed murder during the uprising. When the crowd went up and began to ask Pilate the customary favour, Pilate answered them, "Do you want me to release for you the king of the Jews?" For he realised it was out of jealousy that the chief priests had handed Jesus over. The chief priests, however, had incited the crowd to demand that he should release Barabbas for them instead. Then Pilate spoke again. "But in that case," he said to them, "what am I to do with the man you call king of the Jews?" They shouted back, "Crucify him!" "Why?" Pilate asked them "What harm has he done?" But they shouted all the louder, "Crucify him!" So Pilate, anxious to placate the crowd, released Barabbas for them and, having ordered Jesus to be scourged, handed him over to be crucified.

The soldiers led him away to the inner part of the palace, that is, the Praetorium, and called the whole cohort together. They dressed him up in purple, twisted some thorns into a crown and put it on him. And they began saluting him, "Hail, king of the Jews!" They struck his head with a reed and spat on him; and they went down on their knees to do him homage. And when they had finished making fun of him, they took off the purple and dressed him in his own clothes.

They led him out to crucify him. They enlisted a passer-by, Simon of Cyrene, father of Alexander and Rufus, who was coming in from the country, to carry his cross. They brought Jesus to the place called Golgotha, which means the place of the skull.

They offered him wine mixed with myrrh, but he refused it. Then they crucified him, and shared out his clothing, casting lots to decide what each should get. It was the third hour when they crucified him. The inscription giving the charge against him read: "The King of the Jews." And they crucified two robbers with him, one on his right and one on his left.

The passers-by jeered at him; they shook their heads and said, "Aha! So you would destroy the

Temple and rebuild it in three days! Then save yourself: come down from the cross!" The chief priests and the scribes mocked him among themselves in the same way. "He saved others," they said "he cannot save himself. Let the Christ, the king of Israel, come down from the cross now, for us to see it and believe." Even those who were crucified with him taunted him.

When the sixth hour came there was darkness over the whole land until the ninth hour. And at the ninth hour Jesus cried out in a loud voice, "Eloi, Eloi, lama sabachthani?" which means, "My God, my God, why have you deserted me?" When some of those who stood by heard this, they said, "Listen, he is calling on Elijah." Someone ran and soaked a sponge in vinegar and, putting it on a reed, gave it him to drink, saying, "Wait and see if Elijah will come to take him down." But Jesus gave a loud cry and breathed his last.

All kneel and pause for a moment.

And the veil of the Temple was torn in two from top to bottom. The centurion, who was standing in front of him, had seen how he had died, and he said, "In truth this man was a son of God."

The Gospel of the Lord.
Praise to you, Lord Jesus Christ.

Year C
Gospel (Luke 22:14 – 23:56)

The passion of our Lord Jesus Christ according to Luke.

N. When the hour came Jesus took his place at table, and the apostles with him. And he said to them,

J. "I have longed to eat this passover with you before I suffer; because, I tell you, I shall not eat it again until it is fulfilled in the kingdom of God."

N. Then, taking a cup, he gave thanks and said,

J. "Take this and share it among you, because from now on, I tell you, I shall not drink wine until the kingdom of God comes."

N. Then he took some bread, and when he had given thanks, broke it and gave it to them, saying,

J. "This is my body which will be given for you; do this as a memorial of me."

N. He did the same with the cup after supper, and said,

J. "This cup is the new covenant in my blood which will be poured out for you.

"And yet, here with me on the table is the hand of the man who betrays me. The Son of Man does indeed go to his fate even as it has been decreed, but alas for that man by whom he is betrayed!"

N. And they began to ask one another which of them it could be who was to do this thing.

A dispute arose also between them about which should be reckoned the greatest, but he said to them,

J. "Among pagans it is the kings who lord it over them, and those who have authority over them are given the title Benefactor. This must not happen with you. No; the greatest among you must behave as if he were the youngest, the leader as if he were the one who serves. For who is the greater: the one at table or the one who serves? The one at table, surely? Yet here am I among you as one who serves!

"You are the men who have stood by me faithfully in my trials; and now I confer a kingdom on you, just as my Father conferred one on me: you will eat and drink at my table in my kingdom, and you will sit on thrones to judge the twelve tribes of Israel.

"Simon, Simon! Satan, you must know, has got his wish to sift you all like wheat; but I have prayed for you, Simon, that your faith may not fail, and once you have recovered, you in your turn must strengthen your brothers."

N. He answered,

O. "Lord, I would be ready to go to prison with you, and to death."

N. Jesus replied,

J. "I tell you, Peter, by the time the cock crows today you will have denied three times that you know me."

N. He said to them,

J. "When I sent you out without purse or haversack or sandals, were you short of anything?"

N. They answered,

C. "No."

N. He said to them,

J. "But now if you have a purse, take it: if you have a haversack, do the same; if you have no sword, sell your cloak and buy one, because I tell you these words of scripture have to be fulfilled in me: He let himself be taken for a criminal. Yes, what scripture says about me is even now reaching its fulfilment."

N. They said,

C. "Lord, there are two swords here now."

N. He said to them,

J. "That is enough!"

N. He then left the upper room to make his way as usual to the Mount of Olives, with the disciples following. When they reached the place he said to them,

J. "Pray not to be put to the test."

N. Then he withdrew from them, about a stone's

throw away, and knelt down and prayed, saying,

J. "Father, if you are willing, take this cup away from me. Nevertheless, let your will be done, not mine."

N. Then an angel appeared to him, coming from heaven to give him strength. In his anguish he prayed even more earnestly, and his sweat fell to the ground like great drops of blood.

When he rose from prayer he went to the disciples and found them sleeping for sheer grief. He said to them,

J. "Why are you asleep? Get up and pray not to be put to the test."

N. He was still speaking when a number of men appeared, and at the head of them the man called Judas, one of the Twelve, who went up to Jesus to kiss him. Jesus said,

J. "Judas, are you betraying the Son of Man with a kiss?"

N. His followers, seeing what was happening, said,

C. "Lord, shall we use our swords?"

N. And one of them struck out at the high priest's servant, and cut off his right ear. But at this Jesus spoke,

J. "Leave off! That will do!"

N. And touching the man's ear he healed him.
Then Jesus spoke to the chief priests and

captains of the Temple guard and elders who had come for him. He said,

J. "Am I a brigand that you had to set out with swords and clubs? When I was among you in the Temple day after day you never moved to lay hands on me. But this is your hour; this is the reign of darkness."

N. They seized him then and led him away, and they took him to the high priest's house. Peter followed at a distance. They had lit a fire in the middle of the courtyard and Peter sat down among them, and as he was sitting there by the blaze a servant-girl saw him, peered at him and said,

O. "This person was with him too."

N. But he denied it, saying,

O. "Woman, I do not know him."

N. Shortly afterwards, someone else saw him and said,

O. "You are another of them."

N. But Peter replied,

O. "I am not, my friend."

N. About an hour later, another man insisted, saying,

O. "This fellow was certainly with him. Why, he is a Galilean."

N. Peter said,

O. "My friend, I do not know what you are talking about."

N. At that instant, while he was still speaking, the cock crew, and the Lord turned and looked straight at Peter, and Peter remembered what the Lord had said to him, "Before the cock crows today, you will have disowned me three times." And he went outside and wept bitterly.

Meanwhile the men who guarded Jesus were mocking and beating him. They blindfolded him and questioned him, saying,

C. "Play the prophet. Who hit you then?"

N. And they continued heaping insults on him.

When day broke there was a meeting of the elders of the people, attended by the chief priests and scribes. He was brought before their council, and they said to him,

C. "If you are the Christ, tell us."

N. He replied,

J. "If I tell you, you will not believe me, and if I question you, you will not answer. But from now on, the Son of Man will be seated at the right hand of the Power of God."

N. Then they all said,

C. "So you are the Son of God then?"

N. He answered,

J. "It is you who say I am."

N. They said,

C. "What need of witnesses have we now? We have heard it for ourselves from his own lips."

N. The whole assembly then rose, and they brought him before Pilate.
   They began their accusation by saying,

C. "We found this man inciting our people to revolt, opposing payment of tribute to Caesar, and claiming to be Christ, a king."

N. Pilate put to him this question,

O. "Are you the king of the Jews?"

N. He replied,

J. "It is you who say it."

N. Pilate then said to the chief priests and the crowd,

O. "I find no case against this man."

N. But they persisted,

C. "He is inflaming the people with his teaching all over Judaea; it has come all the way from Galilee, where he started, down to here."

N. When Pilate heard this, he asked if the man were a Galilean; and finding that he came under Herod's jurisdiction he passed him over to Herod who was also in Jerusalem at that time.
   Herod was delighted to see Jesus; he had heard about him and had been wanting for a long time to set eyes on him; moreover, he

was hoping to see some miracle worked by him. So he questioned him at some length; but without getting any reply. Meanwhile the chief priests and the scribes were there, violently pressing their accusations. Then Herod, together with his guards, treated him with contempt and made fun of him; he put a rich cloak on him and sent him back to Pilate. And though Herod and Pilate had been enemies before, they were reconciled that same day.

Pilate then summoned the chief priests and the leading men and the people. He said,

O. "You brought this man before me as a political agitator. Now I have gone into the matter myself in your presence and found no case against him. Nor has Herod either, since he has sent him back to us. As you can see, the man has done nothing that deserves death, so I shall have him flogged and then let him go."

N. But as one man they howled,

C. "Away with him! Give us Barabbas!"

N. This man had been thrown into prison for causing a riot in the city and for murder.

Pilate was anxious to set Jesus free and addressed them again, but they shouted back,

C. "Crucify him! Crucify him!"

N. And for the third time he spoke to them,

O. "Why? What harm has this man done? I have

found no case against him that deserves death, so I shall have him punished and then let him go."

N. But they kept on shouting at the top of their voices, demanding that he should be crucified, and their shouts were growing louder.

Pilate then gave his verdict: their demand was to be granted. He released the man they asked for, who had been imprisoned for rioting and murder, and handed Jesus over to them to deal with as they pleased.

As they were leading him away they seized on a man, Simon from Cyrene, who was coming in from the country, and made him shoulder the cross and carry it behind Jesus. Large numbers of people followed him, and of women too, who mourned and lamented for him. But Jesus turned to them and said,

J. "Daughters of Jerusalem, do not weep for me; weep rather for yourselves and for your children. For the days will surely come when people will say, 'Happy are those who are barren, the wombs that have never borne, the breasts that have never suckled!' Then they will begin to say to the mountains, 'Fall on us!'; to the hills, 'Cover us!' For if men use the green wood like this, what will happen when it is dry?"

N. Now with him they were also leading out two other criminals to be executed.

When they reached the place called The Skull, they crucified him there and the two criminals also, one on the right, the other on the left. Jesus said,

J. "Father, forgive them; they do not know what they are doing."

N. Then they cast lots to share out his clothing. The people stayed there watching him. As for the leaders, they jeered at him, saying,

C. "He saved others; let him save himself if he is the Christ of God, the Chosen One."

N. The soldiers mocked him too, and when they approached to offer him vinegar they said,

C. "If you are the king of the Jews, save yourself."

N. Above him there was an inscription: "This is the King of the Jews."
   One of the criminals hanging there abused him, saying,

O. "Are you not the Christ? Save yourself and us as well."

N. But the other spoke up and rebuked him,

O. "Have you no fear of God at all? You got the same sentence as he did, but in our case we deserved it: we are paying for what we did. But this man has done nothing wrong. Jesus, remember me when you come into your kingdom."

N. He replied,

J. "Indeed, I promise you, today you will be with me in paradise."

N. It was now about the sixth hour and, with the sun eclipsed, a darkness came over the whole land until the ninth hour. The veil of the Temple was torn right down the middle; and when Jesus had cried out in a loud voice, he said,

J. "Father, into your hands I commit my spirit."

N. With these words he breathed his last.

All kneel and pause for a moment.

> When the centurion saw what had taken place, he gave praise to God and said,

O. "This was a great and good man."

N. And when all the people who had gathered for the spectacle saw what had happened, they went home beating their breasts.

All his friends stood at a distance; so also did the women who had accompanied him from Galilee, and they saw all this happen.

Then a member of the council arrived, an upright and virtuous man named Joseph. He had not consented to what the others had planned and carried out. He came from Arimathaea, a Jewish town, and he lived in the hope of seeing the kingdom of God. This man went to Pilate and asked for the body of Jesus. He then took it down, wrapped it in a shroud and put him in a tomb which was hewn in stone in which no one had yet been laid. It was Preparation Day and the sabbath was imminent.

Meanwhile the women who had come from Galilee with Jesus were following behind. They took note of the tomb and of the position of the body.

Then they returned and prepared spices and ointments. And on the sabbath day they rested, as the law required.

The Gospel of the Lord.
Praise to you, Lord Jesus Christ.

This shorter alternative may be read instead:

Gospel (Luke 23:1-49)

The passion of our Lord Jesus Christ according to Luke.

The elders of the people and the chief priests and scribes rose, and they brought Jesus before Pilate.

They began their accusation by saying, "We found this man inciting our people to revolt, opposing payment of tribute to Caesar, and claiming to be Christ, a king." Pilate put to him this question, "Are you the king of the Jews?" "It is you who say it" he replied. Pilate then said to the chief priests and the crowd, "I find no case against this man." But they persisted, "He is inflaming the people with his teaching all over Judaea; it has come all the way from Galilee, where he started, down to here." When Pilate heard this, he asked if the man were a Galilean; and finding that he came under Herod's jurisdiction he passed him over to Herod who was also in Jerusalem at that time.

Herod was delighted to see Jesus; he had heard about him and had been wanting for a long time to set eyes on him; moreover, he was hoping to see some miracle worked by him. So he questioned him at some length; but without getting any reply. Meanwhile the chief priests and the scribes were there, violently pressing their accusations. Then Herod, together with his guards, treated him with contempt and made fun of him; he put a rich cloak on him and sent him back to Pilate. And though Herod and Pilate had been enemies before, they were reconciled that same day.

Pilate then summoned the chief priests and the leading men and the people. "You brought this man before me", he said, "as a political agitator. Now I have gone into the matter myself in your presence and found no case against the man in respect of all the charges you bring against him. Nor has Herod either, since he has sent him back to us. As you can see, the man has done nothing that deserves death, so I shall have him flogged and then let him go." But as one man they howled, "Away with him! Give us Barabbas!" (This man had been thrown into prison for causing a riot in the city and for murder.)

Pilate was anxious to set Jesus free and addressed them again, but they shouted back, "Crucify him! Crucify him!" And for the third time he spoke to them, "Why? What harm has this man done? I have found no case against him that deserves death, so I shall have him punished and then let him go." But they kept on shouting at the top of their voices, demanding that he should be crucified, and their shouts were growing louder.

Pilate then gave his verdict: their demand was to be granted. He released the man they asked for, who had been imprisoned for rioting and murder, and handed Jesus over to them to deal with as they pleased.

As they were leading him away they seized on a man, Simon from Cyrene, who was coming in from the country, and made him shoulder the cross and carry it behind Jesus. Large numbers of people followed him, and of women too, who mourned and lamented for him. But Jesus turned to them and said, "Daughters of Jerusalem, do not weep for me; weep rather for yourselves and for your children. For the days will surely come when people will say, "Happy are those who are barren, the wombs that have never borne, the breasts that have never suckled!" Then they will begin to say to the mountains, "Fall on us!"; to the hills, "Cover us!" For if men use the green wood like this, what will happen when it is dry?" Now with him they were also leading out two other criminals to be executed.

When they reached the place called The Skull, they crucified him there and the two criminals also, one on the right, the other on the left. Jesus said, "Father, forgive them; they do not know what they are doing." Then they cast lots to share out his clothing.

The people stayed there watching him. As for the leaders, they jeered at him. "He saved others," they said, "let him save himself if he is the Christ of God, the Chosen One." The soldiers mocked him too and when they approached to offer him vinegar they said, "If you are the king of the Jews, save yourself." Above him there was an inscription: "This is the King of the Jews."

One of the criminals hanging there abused him. "Are you not the Christ?" he said. "Save yourself and us as well." But the other spoke up and rebuked him. "Have you no fear of God at all?" he said. "You got the same sentence as he did, but in our case we deserved it: we are paying for what we did. But this man has done nothing wrong. Jesus," he said, "remember me when you come into your kingdom." "Indeed, I promise you," he replied, "today you will be with me in paradise."

It was now about the sixth hour and, with the sun eclipsed, a darkness came over the whole land until the ninth hour. The veil of the Temple was torn right down the middle; and when Jesus had cried out in a loud voice, he said, "Father, into your hands I commit my spirit." With these words he breathed his last.

All kneel and pause for a moment.

When the centurion saw what had taken place, he gave praise to God and said, "This was a great and good man." And when all the people who had gathered for the spectacle saw what had happened, they went home beating their breasts.

All his friends stood at a distance; so also did the women who had accompanied him from Galilee, and they saw all this happen.

The Gospel of the Lord.
Praise to you, Lord Jesus Christ.

A brief homily may follow. A period of silence may also be observed.

The Apostles' Creed

**I believe in God,
the Father almighty,
Creator of heaven and earth,
and in Jesus Christ, his only Son, our Lord,**

(all bow during the next two lines)

**who was conceived by the Holy Spirit,
born of the Virgin Mary,
suffered under Pontius Pilate,
was crucified, died and was buried;
he descended into hell;
on the third day he rose again from the dead;
he ascended into heaven,
and is seated at the right hand of God the Father almighty;
from there he will come to judge the living and the dead.**

**I believe in the Holy Spirit,
the holy catholic Church,
the communion of saints,
the forgiveness of sins,
the resurrection of the body,
and life everlasting. Amen.**

The Prayer of the Faithful
(Bidding Prayers)

After each intention there is a pause while all pray. This time of silent prayer may be followed by the next intention, or by a response such as:

Lord, in your mercy.
Hear our prayer.

The priest concludes the biddings with a prayer.

THE LITURGY OF THE EUCHARIST

A hymn may be sung, and the bread and wine for the celebration are brought to the altar. The priest offers prayers of blessing. If these are said aloud the people each time acclaim:

Blessed be God for ever.

The priest completes other personal preparatory rites, then all stand as he says:

Pray, brethren (brothers and sisters),
that my sacrifice and yours
may be acceptable to God,
the almighty Father.

**May the Lord accept the sacrifice at your hands
for the praise and glory of his name,
for our good
and the good of all his holy Church.**

Prayer over the Offerings

Through the Passion of your Only Begotten Son, O Lord,
may our reconciliation with you be near at hand,
so that, though we do not merit it by our own deeds,
yet by this sacrifice made once for all,
we may feel already the effects of your mercy.
Through Christ our Lord.
Amen.

The Eucharistic Prayer

The Lord be with you.
And with your spirit.

Lift up your hearts.
We lift them up to the Lord.

Let us give thanks to the Lord our God.
It is right and just.

It is truly right and just, our duty and our salvation,
always and everywhere to give you thanks,
Lord, holy Father, almighty and eternal God,
through Christ our Lord.

For, though innocent, he suffered willingly for sinners
and accepted unjust condemnation to save the guilty.
His Death has washed away our sins,
and his Resurrection has purchased our justification.

And so, with all the Angels,
we praise you, as in joyful celebration we acclaim:

Holy, Holy, Holy Lord God of hosts.
Heaven and earth are full of your glory.
Hosanna in the highest.
Blessed is he who comes in the name of the Lord.
Hosanna in the highest.

The priest continues with the Eucharistic Prayer. After the words of consecration he says:

The mystery of faith.

**We proclaim your Death, O Lord,
and profess your Resurrection
until you come again.**

or

**When we eat this Bread and drink this Cup,
we proclaim your Death, O Lord,
until you come again.**

or

**Save us, Saviour of the world,
for by your Cross and Resurrection
you have set us free.**

At the conclusion of the Eucharistic Prayer the priest takes the chalice and the paten with the host and, raising both, he sings or says:

Through him, and with him, and in him,
O God, almighty Father,
in the unity of the Holy Spirit,
all glory and honour is yours,
for ever and ever.
Amen.

The Communion Rite
The Lord's Prayer

At the Saviour's command
and formed by divine teaching,
we dare to say:

**Our Father, who art in heaven,
hallowed be thy name;
thy kingdom come,
thy will be done
on earth as it is in heaven.
Give us this day our daily bread,
and forgive us our trespasses,
as we forgive those who trespass against us;
and lead us not into temptation,
but deliver us from evil.**

Deliver us, Lord, we pray,
    from every evil,
graciously grant peace in our days,
that, by the help of your mercy,
we may be always free from sin
and safe from all distress,
as we await the blessed hope
and the coming of our Saviour,
    Jesus Christ.

**For the kingdom,
the power and the glory are yours
now and for ever.**

The Peace

Lord Jesus Christ,
who said to your Apostles:
Peace I leave you, my peace I give you;
look not on our sins,
but on the faith of your Church,
and graciously grant her peace and unity
in accordance with your will.
Who live and reign for ever and ever.
Amen.

The peace of the Lord be with you always.
And with your spirit.

Let us offer each other the sign of peace.

All offer one another the customary sign of peace, which is an expression of peace, communion and charity.

The Breaking of the Bread

The priest takes the host and breaks it, as the following is sung or said:

Lamb of God, you take away the sins of the world, have mercy on us.
Lamb of God, you take away the sins of the world, have mercy on us.
Lamb of God, you take away the sins of the world, grant us peace.

Invitation to Communion

The priest raises the host and says:

Behold the Lamb of God,
behold him who takes away the sins of the world.
Blessed are those called to the supper of the Lamb.

Lord, I am not worthy
that you should enter under my roof,
but only say the word
and my soul shall be healed.

After the priest has consumed the Body and Blood of Christ, the communicants come forward in reverent procession to receive Communion.

The Communion Antiphon may be said or sung, or a hymn or psalm may be sung, beginning while the priest is receiving the Body of Christ.

Communion Antiphon

**Father, if this chalice cannot pass without my
   drinking it,
your will be done.**

The priest or minister shows the host to each of the communicants, saying:

The Body of Christ.
Amen.

When Communion is ministered under both kinds, the minister of the chalice raises it slightly and shows it to each of the communicants, saying:

The Blood of Christ.
Amen.

After the distribution of Communion, if appropriate, a silence may be observed for a while, or a psalm or other canticle of praise or a hymn may be sung.

Then the priest says:

Let us pray.

Prayer after Communion

Nourished with these sacred gifts,
we humbly beseech you, O Lord,
that, just as through the death of your Son
you have brought us to hope for what we believe,
so by his Resurrection
you may lead us to where you call.
Through Christ our Lord.
Amen.

THE CONCLUDING RITES

Any brief announcements now follow.
Then the dismissal takes place.

The Lord be with you.
And with your spirit.

Solemn Blessing

Bow down for the blessing.

May God, the Father of mercies,
who has given you an example of love
in the Passion of his Only Begotten Son,
grant that, by serving God and your neighbour,
you may lay hold of the wondrous gift of his blessing.
Amen.

So that you may receive the reward of everlasting life from him,
through whose earthly Death
you believe that you escape eternal death.
Amen.

And by following the example of his self-abasement,
may you possess a share in his Resurrection.
Amen.

And may the blessing of almighty God,
the Father, and the Son, ✚ and the Holy Spirit,
come down on you and remain with you for ever.
Amen.

or

Prayer over the People

Look, we pray, O Lord, on this your family,
for whom our Lord Jesus Christ
did not hesitate to be delivered into the hands of the wicked
and submit to the agony of the Cross.
Who lives and reigns for ever and ever.
Amen.

And may the blessing of almighty God,
the Father, and the Son, ✠ and the Holy Spirit,
come down on you and remain with you for ever.
Amen.

Dismissal

Then the deacon or the priest says:

Go forth, the Mass is ended.

or

Go and announce the Gospel of the Lord.

or

Go in peace, glorifying the Lord by your life.

or

Go in peace.

Thanks be to God.